Deliver Me from Negative Self Talk

Faithful Words You Should Say When You Talk To Yourself

Lynn R. Davis

PUBLISHED BY: Lynn R Davis

Be the first to know when my books are free. Visit: LynnRDavis.com today to register your email address.

Talking Guide Example:

Don't Declare : "My entire body aches. I'm just falling apart!"

Do Declare: Sickness and disease shall not lord over me.

D0465377

Table of Contents

Preface

Satan deliberately attacked Job's family, his possessions, and his physical health.

Sometimes the problems we face are direct attacks from the enemy. But other times, we have ourselves to blame. We curse ourselves by declaring words of doom and death.

Words should be chosen carefully, because they have power to give life and to destroy it.

Negative self-talk is conceived in the mind and birthed through our speech. But just as negative seeds produce a negative harvest, so will the seeds of God's word, planted in a faithful heart, produce an abundant harvest of blessings.

Introduction:

Proverbs 18: 21 says, "Life and death are in the power of the tongue." Simply put, the words we declare will either give life or cause death. Where did we get this powerful gift?

From our Father that's where. Just as God created the heavens and the earth by speaking words, we too can create the life we desire for ourselves.

Here's an easy formula to remember:

MEDITATION + DECLARATION = MANIFESTATION

If you want something to happen in your life, speak it into existence and then act on your faith. Instead of talking about how terrible your relationship is, confess that the relationship is Godly and all is well.

Does this mean that you can "name it and claim it?" No that's not what I am saying at all. There is more to breakthrough and manifestation than claiming it. What I am encouraging you to do is believe. Believe that God wants you to live a blessed and victorious life at whatever level you are.

Believe that God still can and will do miracles. Believe that God loves you enough to care about what you are going through and will move on your behalf if you have faith to believe.

Your words matter. Your thoughts matter. Your actions are crucial. This book covers your speech. It deals with the negative thoughts that bombard your mind when you're going through hell, your friends and family are MIA, and you can't see how you're going to make it.

The negative thoughts tempt you to say what you see. I'm asking you to challenge yourself. Don't say what you see, declare what you desire.

If you want something to manifest in your life, you have the power to speak it into existence. The opposite is also true. The things that you don't want in your life can also manifested because of your continuous negative self talk. Instead of talking about how terrible your life is or how miserable your relationship is, why not say what you want? Why not confess that your partner has a Godly attitude and all is well?

Shift your focus from your problem to God's promises. Faith pleases God (Hebrews 11:6). And your faith comes by hearing the word of God (Romans 10:17).

Be Careful What You Say

We are made in the image of God and "By the word of the LORD were the heavens made; and all the host of them by the breath of his." (Psalm 33:6)

Just as the Lord created the world with words, the words you speak create the world that you experience. That's why it's important to bridal your tongue especially when you're angry.

"Through faith we understand that the worlds were framed by the word of God, so that things which are seen were not made of things which do." (Hebrews 11:3)

When you are upset or angry, resist the temptation to feed the fire of doom with negative words. No matter how broke you are, don't go around saying, "I'm broke." No matter how rebellious your child seems, resist the urge to say, "You're hopeless!"

Instead, when you face financial challenges say, "All of my needs are met in Jesus' name." When you speak what you want, you are calling it into existence.

Each time your child rebels, administer discipline in love and declare, "The seed of the righteous is blessed!"

Even though it seems that nothing is happening in the natural world, things are changing in the spirit realm.

Your words are a seed planted in the ground. You can't see what's happening. But the chemistry of the ground is changing and the seed is germinating.

Don't get discouraged because you can't see a change in your finances right away. Don't revert to negative self-talk because your child misses curfew again.

Take a deep breath. Know that God is moving. Your faith is pleasing Him and things will change. And like the blossom breaks through the surface of the ground, your prayers will be answered and a breakthrough will spring forth.

And it's only a matter of time before your situation improves. "Calling those things that be not as though they were," is a biblical principal.

Don't be misled. Time is a factor. You don't plant a seed today and see a sprout tomorrow. You've begun a process and that process takes place in stages as described in the Mark 4 Parable of the Sower: "first the blade, then the ear, after that the full corn in the ear."

You have been given the power to sow words and reap a harvest of whatever you have sown. That is why we should be very careful what we say and how we respond to the challenges in our lives.

Once we realize the seriousness of our words, we begin to choose them more carefully. Okay, now that we have our own words under control, let's discuss the next important issue; the words that other people say to us.

Sticks And Stones Break Bones And Words Do Hurt!

Most of the words we hear seem innocent and even humorous. But remember what we said before; words either give life or cause death.

"Sticks and stones may break my bones, but words will never hurt me."

We said it all the time as kids. But the truth is; words *can* hurt. At work I was sharing with a co-worker how I had just been diagnosed with high blood pressure.

His immediate response was, "Be careful. You could stroke out and die." At first I laughed it off. "Boy you're so crazy."

But later that day, I started thinking about what he said. It was true that extreme stress could increase blood pressure and even lead to a stroke.

Had I been experiencing a little numbness - maybe even a little fatigue and dizziness? The negative thoughts started running rampant in my mind.

Honestly, before hearing my friend's "words of wisdom." emphasis on "***dom;***" having a stroke had never entered my mind before he spoke the words.

I meditated on his negativity, and *voilà*! I started experiencing symptoms. Ever heard of hypochondria? The American Century Dictionary defines it as an abnormal anxiety about one's health.

My grandmother was accused of being a hypochondriac. She was always experiencing multiple types of illnesses.

Even though doctors couldn't find anything wrong; bottles of prescriptions lined her dresser. Eighty percent of her day was spent in bed.

Granny only got out of the house for doctor's appointments. Friends and neighbors visited with their stories of doom and gloom. Their words were feeding her fear of death by illness.

If only she had known the power that she had within her to speak health and healing into her life, to control her anxiety, and call forth a sound mind and peace.

Granny had the fiery darts of negativity shooting at her from all directions-both from within and from the gloomy people around her.

What's my point? She meditated on the thoughts and like seeds they took root and produced fear. The fear produced doubt. And doubt murders faith.

The constant meditating on negativity lead to her taking multiple medications, but never to her being healed. As believers we must not allow negativity to overcome us.

Read Paul's instructions to the church: "For the weapons of our warfare are not carnal but mighty in God for pulling down strongholds, casting down arguments and every high thing that exalts itself against the knowledge of God and to bring every thought into captivity" 2 Cor. 10:4-5.

We have to capture bad thoughts and control them with the word of God. The only way to win a spiritual battle is to fight it using spiritual weapons.

"(3) We are human, but we don't wage war as humans do. (4) We use God's mighty weapons, not worldly weapons, to knock down the strongholds of human reasoning and to destroy false arguments." (2 Cor. 10 NLV)

If I hadn't come to myself and remembered that Jesus died that I might have life, I would have meditated my way right into a stroke.

How could this happen?

MEDITATION + DECLARATION = MANIFESTATION

It's a process. First, you see or hear something negative. Next, you think about it or meditate on it (too long).

Then, you start speaking or declaring the negative thing you saw or heard. Finally, the negativity overcomes you and you begin to feel like there is no hope.

No Matter How Bad It Looks Stay Positive

Let's say you're having relationship issues. Like most people, you want to vent. So you talk to your friends about your situation. Of course, as your friends, they're going to take your side.

They begin to say negative things about your situation like, "She's never going to change," "Just leave," "You deserve better." All of these seeds are planted in your mind just waiting to be watered with fear so that they can grow and produce division and dissolution.

You've now developed a totally pessimistic attitude toward that person and your relationship. And if you allow this to go on, the situation will end in pain. What will you do?

Will you fight with spiritual weapons or will you lay down in defeat? You could respond either way.

But let's look at the spiritual approach. First recognize that Satan hates unity and is working to destroy your relationship. Why does he hate unity?

Because God blesses unity!

Read Psalms 133:1 -3. "(v1) Behold how good and how pleasant it is for brethren to dwell together in unity. (v3) It is like the dew of Hermon Descending upon the mountains of Zion' for there the Lord commanded the blessing-Life forevermore."

We've looked at the spiritual approach. So maybe you're wondering what the negative approach look like? Here goes:

You hear your friend's words. You worry about the negative aspects of your relationship. You start speaking negatively. Your relationship ends.

Short and sweet-once again-whatever you meditate on will manifest.

Revisit the formula:

MEDITATION+ DECLARATION= MANIFESTATION.

That's why God wants us to meditate on His word day and night. And Romans 10:17 tells us that "faith comes by hearing, and hearing by the word of God."

Make God's Words Your Words

As believers, we must speak only words of prosperity, health, and power. It takes some practice. But it can be done. Study the word and meditate on God's promises.

Soon, instead of words of despair flowing from your lips, you will begin to flood your life with God's perfect will! And what started out as practice will be as common as breathing!

Say the formula aloud:

MEDITATION + DECLARATION= MANIFESTATION

1- Words You Should Never Declare Over Yourself

Admit it. You talk to yourself.

I talk to myself all the time. I especially do it when I'm zooming around the house. I remind myself, "don't forget the fabric softener" or scold myself, "Lynn, you put it on the list and still forgot to buy it!"

Of course, these are some of the nicer conversations I have with myself.

And most of the time, self talk is pretty harmless. No one gets offended and nobody gets hurt.

But when a situation is more serious than staticky underwear or crusty oven racks, things change; the voices of panic and fear take over.

Like the day you blow a job interview, lose a loved one, or get devastating news from the doctor. The voices change and innocent self talk turns negative and critical.

We make comments like, "I give up. I can't do it," "I can't go on without them," and "I'll be dead in six months."

Negative thoughts are spiritually impure and must be filtered. The word of God is your filter. Any such thought that makes you feel defeated, hurt, or insufficient is a **LIE** and must be filtered through the word of God.

Study for knowledge. Seek understanding. Pray for wisdom. Find out what the bible says about your situation. Remember, "Seek and you will find."

Your goal is to get to the truth. It is the truth that will set you free!

Your Personal Speaking Guide

Don't say: My entire body aches. I'm just falling apart!
Do Say: Sickness and disease shall not lord over me.

Don't say: I am so exhausted. I really don't feel like doing anything today.
Do Say: I can do all things through Christ who strengthens me

Don't say: This headache is killing me!
Do Say: Headache, I resist you in the name of Jesus and by his stripes I am healed and made whole.

Don't say: I can't do that. I'm too scared. What if I fail?
Do Say: I am courageous. God has not given me a spirit of fear but of a sound mind, power and love.

Don't say: I'm always broke.
Do Say: I am abundantly supplied. God is supplying all of my needs according to his riches in glory.

Don't say: I am so depressed.
Do Say: I have the mind of Christ and the peace of God that surpasses all understanding.

Don't say: I just can't stop this bad habit.
Do Say: I am not tempted or tried above that which I am able to overcome. I am more than a conqueror.

Don't say: Everyone in my family has this problem. It's hereditary, so I will probably have the same problems too.
Do Say: Christ redeemed me from the curse, being made a curse himself. I am delivered out of every affliction.

Don't say: I don't like people. I'd rather be alone, besides people are mean.
Do Say: I have the compassion of Christ in my heart and I love all people.

Don't say: I'll never meet this deadline. My work is overwhelming me, there's no way that I can meet the demands of this job.
Do Say: I have the grace to overcome every obstacle. God is giving me wisdom to solve every problem that I am faced with.

Don't Say: I'm happy with what I have. Why should I want more?
Do Say: Jesus came that I might have abundant life. I am blessed to be a blessing to others.

Don't say: I will never get married. No one wants to marry me.
Do Say: God is preparing me for marriage and he is raising up the perfect mate for me.

Don't Say: God is not answering my prayers so maybe he's not listening.
Do Say: God is mindful of me and he hears me when I pray.

Don't Say: Everything is getting on my nerves and I am going crazy!
Do Say: I will think only of things that are lovely, good, just, and have good report so that the peace of God dwells in me.

Don't say: I'm so angry. I will never be able to forgive.
Do Say: The joy of the Lord is my strength. My heart is filled with the compassion of Christ and I forgive those who trespass against me.

Don't say: My company is going to have a reduction in force. I don't know what I'm going to do if I get laid off.
Do Say: When one door closes God has to open another door.

Don't say: I am lonely. I wish I had someone to in my life.
Do Say: I am complete in Christ. I am never lonely because he is always with me.

Don't say: Things will never get better. I may as well give up.
Do Say: Eyes haven't seen what God has prepared for me and in due season I shall reap, if I faint not.

Don't say: The weather is terrible. I hope I don't have an accident.
Do Say: The angels of the Lord are encamped around me and no hurt or harm shall come near me.

Don't say: I'm too old to change. You can't teach old dogs new tricks.
Do Say: I am a new creature. Old things have passed away.

Don't Say: Everyone else is doing it, why shouldn't I?
Do Say: God has called me out of darkness and into his marvelous light. I am in this world but I am not of this world.

Don't say: I can't help gossiping. My friends encourage it.
Do Say: I will not participate in gossip. Corrupt communication brings destruction.

Don't say: No one cares about me!
Do Say: God loves me and he is Jehovah-Shammah (The Lord Is There)

2-Words You Should Never Speak About Others

As a mother of a recovering addict, I know this principle is a tough one. When I first found out that my son was smoking pot in high school I lost it.

I used words I've never used in my life. I was so angry you could have fried on egg on my head!

I was disappointed in him. Angry that I'd missed the signs and appalled that the enemy had the nerve to go after my child. Not my son! (Maybe that's a book for another time.)

Every chance I got I shared my disgust and contempt for his rebellion. I told family and coworkers how much trouble he was getting into and how many times he'd been arrested.

I complained and lamented till I was out of breath, then had the nerve to pray to God for change. What I should have been doing was praying for him, with him, and speaking words of promise over his life. While keeping my mouth closed about what was happening.

The more negatively I spoke about his habits and his choices, the more he backed away from me and toward the rebellion. It wasn't until I took my negative thoughts into captivity and changed my words, that I began to see change and have been blessed to witness his deliverance.

Learn from my mistakes. Don't speak negativity over the people in your life. If you truly care about them and want to reconcile the relationship, replace your negative perceptions and comments with the word of God.

Remember, **"For our struggle is not against human opponents, but against rulers, authorities, cosmic powers in the darkness around us..."** (Ephesians 6:12)

Your Personal Speaking Guide

Don't say: My supervisor hates me, my co-workers are messy; I hate this job!
Do Say: I love those who hate me and I will do well to those who misuse me. No weapon formed against me shall prosper. The battle is the Lord's.

Don't say: My children do not listen to a word that I say. They are just bad.
Do Say: My child is a blessing from the lord. My child obeys the word of God and honors his mother and father.

Don't say: My husband is lazy and worthless. I don't know why I married him.
Do Say: My husband is a righteous man of God and he loves me like Christ loves the church.

Don't say: My in-laws are incorrigible and they are making my life miserable.
Do Say: My in-laws are transformed by the renewing of their mind. I am an example for them and they will see my good works and glorify the Father in heaven.

Don't say: People in church are cruel. I'm never going to church again.
Do Say: God has many great churches and he is revealing to me the church that I should attend.

Don't say: My child makes terrible grades in school. They will never amount to anything.
Do Say: God has a purpose for my child. My child is royal

priesthood and has the wisdom of Daniel and the favor of God and man. My child is empowered to prosper.

Don't Say: Why do they behave that way? They're just crazy.
Do Say: Christ alone is perfect.

3- Words You Should Never Allow Others to Say About You

Some people are just plain negative. That's all there is to it. But you don't have to allow them to discourage you. Regardless of who they are or how close they may be to us.

Sometimes the people closest to you are the ones who will be the least supportive and the most negative.

You're all excited about your new goal and you share it with your significant other, brother, sister, or BFF and you're met with negativity.

That's the last thing you expected. How are you supposed to process that? What do you do?

You ignore negative people. That's what you do.

I deal with people and their toxic comments all the time regarding my health and weight loss goals.

Anyone who knows me is aware that I'm an advocate of health and fitness. You would think people would appreciate that, right?

Wrong!

I hear comments all the time like, "You're going to be too skinny." "You don't need to lose weight," or "I can't eat like that. I love food too much," on and on...

Did I let that stop me from dropping 4 jean sizes and getting healthy? No. I did not. And I will not. I prefer not spending hundreds of dollars a year on high blood pressure pills and asthma pumps - thank you very much.

You see, I'm fully aware that negative people are speaking from the depths of their own insecurity and self-doubt.

So I brush it off.

That's what I want to encourage you to do as well. When you decide to improve yourself, there will be people who will say and do things to discourage you.

I encourage you to shake those negative people off. Realize they are only projecting their lack of discipline and lack of motivation on to you.

"Hurting people hurt people." I don't know who said that, but it is certainly a true statement.

Some people are unhappy with themselves and they're jealous of your drive and commitment to self-improvement. *How dare you improve your quality of life? Who do you think you are?*

You can't please negative people. They are unhappy no matter what. They speak negatively no matter what. They gossip about you when you fail and they rain on your parade when you succeed.

There's no pleasing them. So stop trying! Simply smile and keep it moving.

You have goals. Don't let negative people deter you. Stay focused and you will succeed.

"Let no corrupt communication proceed out of your mouth, but that which is good to the use of edifying, that it may minister grace unto the hearers." (Ephesians 4:29)

If the words that people are speaking over you don't uplift

you or encourage you to do better, then you should never receive them as truth.

Your Personal Speaking Guide

What they say: You poor thing.
Response: I am blessed and I have the grace to overcome anything!

What they say: How do you plan to acquire that? You don't make enough.
Response: I am abundantly supplied. I am not moved by what I see. It's only temporary.

What they say: That's a terrible sickness; you could die from it.
Response: I am healed. I shall live and not die.

What they say: You don't look well. Are you sick?
Response: I have divine health. I resist sickness in the name of Jesus.

What they say: Yeah right, do you really believe you're going to pull that off?
Response: I can do all things through Christ who strengthens me.

What they say: If I were you, I would be so depressed.
Response: God has not given me the spirit of fear, but of a sound mind, power, and love.

What they say: I could never give that much money to the church. I have bills to pay.
Response: When I give, God causes men to give to me, good measure, press down, shaken together and running over. God supplies all of my needs according to his riches in glory.

What they say: I don't believe in anything that I can't see.
Response: Without faith it is impossible to please God. I receive the promised of God through faith.

What they say: Don't you get tired of cooking, cleaning and taking care of everyone else?
Response: I have the grace to care for the family that God has blessed me with.

4-Words You Should Never Speak About God

God Is Not Angry With You

One of the most difficult things for us to believe as Christians is that God is not mad at us. We condemn ourselves because of our past sins or even our present mistakes.

The danger in believing that you serve an **angry God** is that you will begin to feel you do not deserve God's goodness or His blessings. In turn you will begin to doubt and have fear.

While we don't condone sin or even encourage it, we do know that the bible tells us in Romans 8 "... *there is no condemnation for those who belong to Christ Jesus...*"

I posted a word of encouragement on my Facebook page that I believe applies to this chapter...

"Regardless of disagreements among siblings and family, when an outsider threatens a family member, we rise against that attacker to protect them. Though your actions don't always please God, when the enemy threatens to destroy you, God raises a standard against him to protect you. You have protection. Not because you do everything right, but because you are in God's family. Receive it by faith."

You are part of the family of God. He loves you and wants to protect you. Here are some daily confessions based on Romans 8 and Isaiah 54.

Meditating on these truths will help you to address your

feelings of condemnation and fears of inadequacy because you incorrectly believe that God is angry with you:

- I have an unconditional covenant with God.
- God loves me and He has reconciled me unto himself.
- God is not angry with me. He loves me.
- The mountains and the hills will pass away before God's covenant promise to love me and give me peace can ever be broken.
- God has sworn never to rebuke me or to be angry with me.
- God's covenant of peace will never leave me.
- God's unfailing love and peace for me will never be shaken.
- My righteousness is of the Lord. I am not condemned. I am loved by God.
- Make these confessions daily and know that God loves you regardless of your past, present, or future mistakes. Seek to do good and please Him with your life.

Allow His love to fill your heart and overflow in your life. You do not serve an angry God.

Meditate on Isaiah 54: 10, "Though the mountains be shaken and the hills be removed, yet my unfailing love for you will not be shaken nor my covenant of peace be removed, says the LORD, who has compassion on you." NIV

You serve a loving God. Hills will be removed and mountains shaken before God's love will ever be taken away from you or His covenant with you broken. Believe that. Receive it and walk in victory.

That said, here are a few examples of words you should never speak about God.

- God Doesn't Love Me.
- God is too busy for my problems.
- My problems are too big for God.
- I'm alone. God is not there.
- God can't heal my disease.
- God is going to punish me for my sins.

These are lies, lies, lies; all lies.

The Devil is a liar. He is the "Father of Lies" (John 8:44)

Satan is destined to eternal damnation. He is damned. And he wants to take as many lost souls with him as he possibly can.

Don't let the bad things in life make you believe God doesn't love you.

God is love. And God loves us-with all of our issues and faults. Jehovah is not waiting to condemn you or to punish you. He wants to bless you.

He's waiting to help you and heal the hurt. It doesn't matter how much wrong you've done. Or how many mistakes you've made or will make.

He only wants to bless you. He is mindful of you and no human could ever love you as much as He does!

God is your provider, peace, and healer. He wants the best for you. And you have to get into the habit of talking like it.

One thing that will help is meditating on the names of God. Learning who He is will help you understand His character and how much He loves and wants you to succeed in life.

5- Knowing God's Loving Character

"O LORD, our Lord, How excellent is Your name in all the earth…" Psalm 8:1

When you know who God is, you can't help but feel comforted and empowered. Everything that you could possibly need is in the Father.

He IS whatever you need Him to be. And He is waiting for you to come to Him.

Whatever you need, God IS! God told Moses in Exodus, "I am that I am." Don't put limits on God's ability to heal your body or repair your broken heart.

God loves you and wants you to be prosperous in every area of your life.

Before you allow someone to tell you that God doesn't love you or that He cannot help you, remember the words, "I am that I am."

He is love, provision, protection, peace, healing, etc. The list goes on and on. Let's take a look at some of the most common characteristics of God our Father:

Names of Jehovah God

Adonai: My Master

El Elyon: The Most High God

El Olam: The Everlasting Father

El Roi: My God Sees All

El Shaddai: My All-Sufficient God

Elohim: My Creator

Jehovah-Jireh: The LORD my Provider

Jehovah-Mekoddishkem: The LORD Who sanctifies me

Jehovah-Nissi: The LORD My Banner

Jehovah-Raah: The LORD My Shepherd

Jehovah-Rapha: The LORD That Heals me

Jehovah-Sabaoth: The LORD of Hosts

Jehovah-Shalom: The LORD my Peace

Jehovah-Shammah: The LORD Is Always There

Jehovah-Tsidkenu: The LORD my Righteousness

God is your creator. He loves you. He wants to provide for you. His desire is to heal you and bring you peace in your storms.

You are righteous because of His son Jesus. And He is always with you even at this moment.

There is no need to speak doom and gloom. God has a good plan for your life. The problems you are facing come from the enemy, not the Father (Jeremiah 29:11).

When you know God, you know His nature. By nature, God is love. And that love is unconditional for believers in Jesus Christ.

I hope that you've been blessed. And I could say that this is the end, but it's not; it's only the beginning. Go forth. "Call those things that be not as though they were." (Romans 4:17)

Choose your words carefully from this day forward. Use them to create a life that you enjoy living.

Remember:

**MEDITATION + DECLARATION=
MANIFESTATION**

Dismiss negative thoughts, words, and feelings. Study your Father's character. Meditate on His word. Declare it. And watch your life change for the better.

6-Daily Inspiration and Scripture Meditation

Ever heard the saying, "What's in you will come out?" It's a true saying.

The only way that we can consistently speak faith-filled words is if those words are "in us" or abundant in our hearts. Matthew 12:34, "For out of the abundance of the heart the mouth speaks."

And for God's word to flourish in our hearts, we must sow seeds of the word through daily prayer, mediation, and study.

The word of God in our hearts takes root and produces a bumper crop of manifestation and breakthrough. So that when we open our mouths to speak, faith-filled words will overflow from it.

Actively seek God's guidance and practice speaking faith-filled words daily. It may feel forced or "fake" at first. And you may be tempted to give up, but please don't.

The pages that follow include 7 days of inspiration and scripture meditation. During your study time meditate on them and pray for understanding.

Ask the Holy Spirit to reveal the value and meaning to you for your life and to show you the areas you need to strengthen.

Matthew 7: 7 - *"Ask, and it shall be given you; seek, and ye shall find; knock, and it shall be opened unto you:"*

DAY 1

Scripture Meditation:

Proverbs 18:21 - "Death and life are in the power of the tongue: and they that love it shall eat the fruit thereof."

Thought for today:

Your words can kill or give life. And there are consequences for both. Today make an effort to speak words that give life and hope for a new beginning to a coworker, friend or family member.

Inspirational Quote:

"A helping word to one in trouble is often like a switch on a railroad track an inch between wreck and smooth, rolling prosperity."

-Henry Ward Beecher

DAY 2

Scripture Meditation:

Proverbs 21:23(NLT) - "Watch your tongue and keep your mouth shut, and you will stay out of trouble."

Thought for today:

If you can't say something nice, don't say anything at all." We don't always have to talk. Sometimes, it's better to keep quiet, especially to avoid starting trouble. If your words will cause confusion don't just blurt them out. Let the Holy Spirit guide you. "God is not the author of confusion but of peace," (1 Corinthians 14:33).

Inspirational Quote:

"If a sudden jar can cause me to speak an impatient, unloving word, then I know nothing of Calvary love. For a cup brimful of sweet water cannot spill even one drop of bitter water, however suddenly jolted."

-Amy Carmichael

DAY 3

Scripture Meditation:

1 Corinthians 2:16 (NLT) - "Who can know the Lord's thoughts? Who knows enough to teach them? But we understand these things, for we have the mind of Christ."

Thought for today:

As a believer you have access to God's thoughts-through His Son, His word and His Spirit. As we spend time with God, our relationship with Him matures. And we begin to gain insight and understanding concerning His good plans for our lives. Pray and believe for the mind of Christ. Then allow God's thoughts to lead your actions.

Inspirational Quote:

"We need men so possessed by the Spirit of God that God can think His thoughts through our minds, that He can plan His will through our actions, that He can direct His strategy of world evangelization through His Church."

-Alan Redpath

DAY 4

Scripture Mediation:

Matthew 21:22 (ESV) - "And whatever you ask in prayer, you will receive, if you have faith."

Thought for today:

There will be times when it seems impossible to overcome what you face. With God nothing is impossible. Your faith is the key to overcoming. Don't meditate on doubtful thoughts or speak doubtful words. Doubt turns to unbelief. And it is unbelief that drives a wedge between you and your promised victory. Stand fast on God's word. His word cannot fail.

Inspirational Quote:

"Daily living by faith on Christ is what makes the difference between the sickly and the healthy Christian, between the defeated and the victorious saint."

-A.W.Pink

DAY 5

Scripture Meditation:

Joshua 1: 8 - "This Book of the Law shall not depart from your mouth, but you shall meditate on it day and night, so that you may be careful to do according to all that is written in it. For then you will make your way prosperous, and then you will have good success."

Thought for today:

We are no longer under the law, but covered by grace. However, I believe the principle is that we should not make the mistake of waiting for God to bring us success. He has already blessed us with the greatest success conduit - His son Jesus Christ. To receive the success that is promised to us we must first receive Jesus into our lives as Lord and savior. Then by faith believe that we have also received salvation, healing, prosperity, and wholeness. Meditate on the promises in God's word. Learn them. Believe them. Declare them. And then you "will have good success."

Inspirational Quote:

"The foundation stones for a balanced success are honesty, character, integrity, faith, love and loyalty."

-Zig Ziglar

Day 6

Scripture Meditation:

Isaiah 26:3 – 4 - "You keep him in perfect peace whose mind is stayed on you, because he trusts in you. Trust in the Lord forever, for the Lord God is an everlasting rock:"

Thought for today:

As the hymn says, we often forfeit our peace because we fail to take our problems to God. God wants us to cast our cares on him. Not our unbelieving neighbors, disgruntled coworkers, or pessimistic family members. Though everything around you seems to be falling apart, take heart in knowing that God's word is not. It is solid as an everlasting rock. His word and His love will never fade. He is a part of you. And that part of you is indestructible. It's the part of your life that rebuilds, restores, and resurrects! Nothing is impossible with God.

Inspirational Scripture:

"You were made by God and for God and until you understand that, life will never make sense."

Rick Warren

Day 7

Scripture Meditation:

1 John 4:4 - "Because greater is He that is in you than He that is in the world."

Thought for today:

The word and Jesus are one. "In the beginning was the word. The word was God and the word was with God." (John 1:1) Jesus lives in you. And He that lives in you is greater and more powerful than any obstacle you face in the world. Don't look down at your problems. Look up at the promise. Your help comes from the Lord and He is high and lifted up, just as your countenance should be. Keep your head up.

Inspirational Quote:

"If there be anything that can render the soul calm, dissipate its scruples and dispel its fears, sweeten its sufferings by the anointing of love, impart strength to all its actions, and spread abroad the joy of the Holy Spirit in its countenance and words, it is this simple and childlike repose in the arms of God."

-S.D. Gordon

*Note: The remaining devotionals were previously part of a now **unpublished** title, "I Might Bend but I Won't Break"*

DAY 8 You Are Indestructible

We are troubled on every side, yet not distressed; we are perplexed, but not in despair; Persecuted, but not forsaken; cast down, but not destroyed. 2 Corinthians 4: 8-9

This is one of those scriptures that you absolutely should memorize. "Cast down but not destroyed" always pops into my mind whenever I am going through a tough time. Those words ground me. They make me stop and think about who I am and whose I am. Greater is He that is in me than He that is in the world. There's something about knowing that the world may throw you down, but they cannot completely annihilate you. In Christ you are invincible. Have you ever known people who seem to bounce back no matter what type of situation they go through? Those are people who don't give into the lies that they are destroyed for good.

That's why I like reading comeback stories. They are inspiring. They are motivating. They are examples of 2 Corinthians 4:8-9. They know that they cannot be destroyed because they have a power source on the inside that is indestructible. Our power source is the Holy Spirit and for the believer even death leads to eternal life. Trouble may be coming at you from every direction, but don't give up on the power of Jesus that lives in you. Christ has overcome the world. Use your faith. At our weakest God is His strongest.

There is nothing that can put us in a state of anguish or agony. You physical body may experience extreme stress and fatigue to the point of giving out, but your spirit is stronger than ever. That is where you need to gather your strength from. Not from you physical body, your BFF, or your family, but from the Christ that lives in you. So many things happen in life. We never know what to expect from one day to the next. But we do know that god is the same yesterday, today and forever. His power is the same today, tomorrow, and for eternity. Life isn't always fair, but we can't let the unfair things that happen to us cause us to lose faith in God. We have everlasting life in Christ Jesus. And because we are a part of the body, we cannot be destroyed. Our Lord is always with us.

Life can be a maze of problems and trying to figure out which way to go can make you feel like there is no chance of ever getting out of the hell that you are experiencing. But God has assured us that, "many are the afflictions of the righteous but the Lord will deliver us from them all." There is always hope for the believer.

"Life is a bowl of cherries. Some cherries are rotten while others are good; its your job to throw out the rotten ones and forget about them while you enjoy eating the ones that are good! There are two kinds of people: those who choose to throw out the good cherries and wallow in all the rotten ones, and those who choose to throw out all the rotten ones and savor all the good ones."

DAY 9 Nothing Has Power Over You

In the coming days, no weapon turned against you will succeed. You will silence every voice raised up to accuse you. These benefits are enjoyed by the servants of the Lord' their vindication will come from me. I, the Lord have spoken! (LASB)Isaiah 54:17

I like the way this verse ends in the Life Application Study Bible, "I the Lord have spoken!" The Lord has assured us that no weapon that forms against us will succeed in destroying us. That means nothing and no one can come against you and ultimately succeed in a way that will cause you irrevocable damage. Even if you lose your home, job, or worse still someone you love, the future still is bright because the Lord your God is an ever present help in the time of trouble. There have been times in my life when people I thought were on my side turned out to be my biggest enemies. It hurt to know that they weren't really on my side, but were rooting for my failure and in some cases even formulating ways to hurt me. But in every situation God blessed me to rise to the top. Even if it seemed that I started out sinking. You can't keep a God-fearing believer down! And in instance the voices of accusers and gossipers was silenced. It may seem that the weapon coming against you is going to destroy you, but take heart in the word. It will not succeed. No matter how bad it looks, God will make it better. It's not over until God says it's over. He will bless you in such a way that they will know He is with you and His glory on your life will shut their mouths once and for all. We serve a God who cares about us. He doesn't want us to get bogged down with trying to get back at anyone or trying to create our own weapons to fight with. He wants us to know that He's got our backs. And because He does, that hurtful act that is being planned against may push you down and seem to get the best of you, but it cannot. Because God said it won't. And He will vindicate you. You don't have to. If you want to do something that gets their goat, love them. The bible says you're heaping hot coals on their head when you do something good for your enemy. Vengeance is the Lord and there is no one who does it better than Him. Change your attitude about what you're going through. You know something that your enemy does not. You know that what they are doing will succeed. You know that God will bless you so well that you will shut their mouths. And you know that vengeance is in God's hands. You have the upper hand.

"What is the difference between an obstacle and an opportunity? Our attitude toward it. Every opportunity has a difficulty, and every difficulty has an opportunity." — J. Sidlow Baxter

DAY 10 He's Here There and Everywhere

"Behold, I am the LORD, the God of all flesh; is anything too difficult for Me?" **Jeremiah 32:27, NASB**

Jeremiah knew the Lords power, he knew God had all power, but he didn't quite understand why God was telling him to purchase a certain area of land that was going to be conquered. The Lord answered Jeremiah's question with a question, "…is anything too difficult for Me?" God is still asking us that today. Often we question what God has instructed us to do because it doesn't make sense. When I was praying about my son and drug addiction, God told me to trust Him and that His ways are not my ways. I didn't understand why He wanted me to do the things He was instructing me to do, but I trusted Him because He is the almighty and nothing is too hard for him- no matter how hard it may seem for me. But we must remember that God would not instruct us to do anything that is going to destroy us. Nor will He send us anywhere that He will not be with us. God is everywhere we need Him to be whenever we need Him. Nothing is too hard for Him. Take heart in the fact that your God is the only true God. And He has ultimate authority. He created the heavens and the earth. There is nothing in the earth that He is not aware of. What you are facing is no surprise to God. The day you were born, he knew what you'd be going through today. It's easy to give into feelings of insecurity and fear. Typically we do so because we are looking at our situation through human eyes. If we don't have the physical strength or means to take care of the problem, then we project that weakness onto God. God is not a man. He does not have the weaknesses that we have. But make no mistake He is well aware of our feelings, emotions, and limitations. Christ Jesus experienced everything that we have experienced and He overcame it.1 Corinthians 10:13 assures us that we are not facing any new temptation. And that God will not let us be tempted beyond what we can bear and on top of that God will provide a way for us to endure. Just like Jeremiah we must take confidence in knowing that God knows what's ahead. He knows that what we will have to endure will only be for a season and that we will come out victorious if we trust that there is nothing impossible for Him to accomplish in our lives.

"If you say you can or you can't you are right either way" – Henry Ford

DAY 11

You Are Made in His Image and He is Great

Yours, LORD, is the greatness and the power and the glory and the majesty and the splendor, for everything in heaven and earth is yours. Yours, LORD, is the kingdom; you are exalted as head over all. (1 Chronicles 29:11)

Don't let your atmosphere determine how you feel about yourself or what your attitude will be. Circumstances change and if you allow outside influences to dictate your attitude it will be changing like the weather. Some days you will be angry other days you may be sad. And only on a few occasions when everything goes your way will you be glad. But how often does EVERYTHING go your way?

To have a winning attitude you must know who your God is. King David knew how awesome and wonderful his God was and he showed that in his prayer of praise. It's not enough just to know how wonderful God is, you have to also remember, that you are created in His image. So if He is wonderful, so are you!

The scripture says everything in heaven and earth is the Lords. Your God owns it all. There is nothing in heaven or on earth that God does not rule over. You serve a mighty God who wants you to walk in victory. Every resource that you need, He is able to supply because He owns it all.

Embrace your inner power. You succeed according to the power of God that works in you. (Ephesians 3:20) You have to own it! Even if you are going through tribulation right now, rejoice and give God praise. Because that tribulation is working in your favor. It's increasing your patience and your faith. Its helping you develop the faith you need to manifest the power of the Almighty that is given to those who believe and receive the Christ Jesus. While you give God praise for His power you should be beaming with self-confidence because that power resides on the inside of you. Your attitude should be that of a winner because there is no way you can lose when the power of the most high God is working in and through you every second of every day. Accept it. Believe it. Act like it is so.

"Cultivate an optimistic mind, use your imagination, always consider alternatives, and dare to believe that you can make possible what others think is impossible."
Rodolfo Costa

DAY 12 He Has Your Back

"Contend, LORD, with those who contend with me; fight against those who fight against me." Psalm 35:1

David prayed to God for justice. He was angry, hurt, and confused. Why were people trying to kill him? What had he done to deserve such horrible treatment? Often times we find ourselves in situations where we don't understand why people are treating us the way that they are. Their actions are unfair and in some cases unjust. God does not want us to feel that we have to accept cruelty from anyone. He promises that He will protect us and deliver us from every affliction (Psalm 34:19). Cruel people cannot break you unless you allow them to. If you don't change the way you respond to their behavior you will stress yourself out and possibly even end up sick. Do what a winner would do. Change your perception. See the cruelty behavior as a challenge, an opportunity. The opportunity to be blessed for doing something that pleases God –loving your enemy. You will experience a sense of victory over the situation when you are able to look at it without getting angry upset and distressed. These emotions are not only unhealthy; they are unproductive and ungodly as they indicate that your faith is weak in that area. Winners allow their behavior to reflect the love of God in the most difficult situations.

There will be times that you will be angry. The bible even speaks of anger, "Be ye **angry**, and **sin not**: let **not** the sun go down upon your wrath:" Ephesians 4:26. Accept that you are angry about the situation. You may even tell God, "Lord I'm angry." But don't stop there. Ask Him to give you peace and guidance as to how you should deal with the problem. But do not let allow the anger to lead to vengeful or self-destructive behavior. David was in a terrible position for a time. He was hurt and angry, but he prayed to God. God came through for David, not right away as David had hoped, but in the end David reined as king. Keep the right attitude. Stay in faith. Go ahead; it's okay to be angry. You're bending when you're angry. But don't break. Don't lose faith and do something that will derail your spiritual walk or cause more damage. Trust that God is faithful. Your deliverance is on the way. And you will reign over your circumstances!

"When you are joyful, when you say yes to life and have fun and project positivity all around you, you become a sun in the center of every constellation, and people want to be near you." — Shannon L. Alder

DAY 13 Aint No Mountain High Enough

Who shall separate us from the love of Christ? Shall trouble or hardship or persecution or famine or nakedness or danger or sword." Romans 8:35

Nothing you're facing can ever separate you from the love of God. It doesn't matter if it's a struggle in your daily life, relationship, on your job or related to your health. These words belong to a very popular secular song: *"Ain't no mountain high enough. Ain't no valley low enough. Ain't no river wide enough to keep me from getting to you."* Thought the song is referring to relationships between men and women, it's a really simplistic way to also think about how God's love is toward us. No matter what in our life is making us bend and causing us to feel like we're about to break, it's nothing that can keep God from coming to our rescue. When I was facing foreclosure, I thought I was going to lose my home. I was afraid. He enveloped me in His love and comforted me reassuring me that no matter what, He would always be there for me. He'd never leave me homeless or forsake me. God worked that situation out for me. He came through. Not because I was a perfect Christian who was living a perfect life, but because I am His child and His love for me is unconditional and everlasting. But even if I'd lost my home, I still would have faith in the power of god's love. Just because we go through difficult times it doesn't mean that we are unloved. Romans 8:34 assures us that Jesus is interceding for us in heaven. Our sins have been removed because of Jesus. Don't let the situation you face make you believe that you have gotten so far away that God's love cannot reach you. He has not abandoned you and He never will-Christ never will. He died for you. There is no greater love. And there is not greater power than the one that dwells in you.

"Always strive to aim for the highest peak of the goals in life you have set, this way if you manage to reach even half way toward a goal, landing in the middle is not such a bad place to end up." — Victoria Addino

DAY 14 Wings Like An Eagle

"But they that wait upon the LORD shall renew their strength; they shall mount up with wings as eagles; they shall run, and not be weary; and they shall walk, and not faint." Isaiah 40:31

Before you can hope to live a victorious life, you must first believe God loves you no matter what and He want wants what is best for you in every situation. When you believe that you will find strength that you didn't know you had. Right now you may be feeling weak and unsure of yourself. That's because you've forgotten that you serve a God that loves you, not because you are perfect, but because His son Jesus Christ has reconcile your relationship with him. You see it is not through your righteousness that you're entitled to victory and blessings; it's through the righteousness of our Lord and Savior Jesus Christ. He bore your sins. You don't have to. Stop beating yourself up and trying to atone for your own sins. Christ has already done that. All you have to do is accept, receive, and believe. There is no sin that you've committed that Christ didn't know about the day He laid His life on the cross for you. You are forgiven. Because you are forgiven, you are entitled to all that heaven has to offer, in Jesus Christ. Knowing that and reminding yourself of it regularly will give you renewed strength. And as you go throughout the day, week, month, you will not become weary, because you know that God's love is stronger than anything you face. Your renewed strength will be as if you have mounted up on wings like an eagle. Eagles are marvelous creatures. They have Wingspans up to 90 inches and can fly at an altitude of 10,000 feet! Imagine yourself soaring high above problems, petty attitudes, and life's most challenging moments. Think of yourself so strong that you can run this race of life without getting tired; and walk through the darkest day without fainting from fear. You can do that when you trust in God and wait on him.

"Hard work does not go unnoticed, and someday the rewards will follow" — Allan Rufus

DAY 15 You Can Be Afraid and Still Be Courageous

"Wait on the LORD: be of good courage, and he shall strengthen thine heart: wait, I say, on the LORD." Psalm 27:14

Courage is not the absence of fear. That is a common mistake that I believe many make. We all experience fear in some form or another. Some fear speaking in public, while others fear flying, or insects. I've been told that I do very well at public speaking. However, I have to admit that it scares me. I always imagine myself making a mistake and everyone pointing and laughing. There are so many things in life that we can be afraid of. The important thing though is to not allow fear to stop you from moving forward. I think that's when we run into problems. That's when we hinder ourselves from succeeding in life. The scripture says be of "good courage". Patience to wait on God requires bravery. When God doesn't seem to be moving as fast as you'd like, you can sometimes become afraid. I know when I was praying for my son during the period that he was battling drug addiction, there was a time when I started to become afraid. God wasn't moving fast enough for me and it seemed my son would surely be lost forever or worse, I'd be planning his funeral. But God wants us to be courageous. Courage will allow us to remain in faith. When He sees that we are brave in Him, then he will strengthen our hearts. Just because we are trembling in fear, doesn't mean we can't still be trusting in faith! Faith pleases God. People who have a winning attitude are brave enough to trust God in their heart even when their mind tells them they should be afraid. Take off those old negative thoughts of fear and put on your new winning attitude of bravery. Ah! It looks good on you!

"A positive attitude may not solve all our problems but that is the only option we have if we want to get out of problems. -Subodh Gupta

DAY 16 Flawed But Faithful

"Hope in the LORD and keep his way. He will exalt you to inherit the land; when the wicked are destroyed, you will see it." Psalm 37:34

The entire 37 Psalm is a motivational read for anyone looking for inspiration. David reminds us that God is always with the righteous ready to protect and provide. Instead of hoping in our careers and people, our hope must be in the Lord. To hope means to have confidence that the outcome of your situation will be a positive one. As believers this is the hope that we have, because of our Lord and Saviors self-sacrifice, our Father in heaven desires to exalt us and give us victory.

It's in this same chapter David says, "I've never seen the righteous forsaken." God cares about us and He has our back in every situation. One thing God asks of us is that we stay on the righteous path. We don't have to be perfect on our journey nor do we have to keep up with other Christians. Our journey is our own. In the natural we have flaws. We can see them in the mirror, but only man is considered with the outward appearance. God looks at the heart. We need only please God with the desires of our hearts and He will honor our efforts. He will protect us and keep us. We don't have to worry about how we're going to make it; we just have to have faith that God will exalt us because of our faithfulness and our right standing through Jesus Christ, not our religious works or flawless personalities.

"Never let go of hope. One day you will see that it all has finally come together. What you have always wished for has finally come to be. You will look back and laugh at what has passed and you will ask yourself... 'How did I get through all of that?" - Unknown.

DAY 17 You Are A Winner!

Watch ye, stand fast in the faith, quit you like men, be strong. (14) And do everything in love. 1 Corinthians 16:13-14

Paul loved the Corinthians. He wanted them to succeed. In his letter to them, he encouraged them to remember the gospel that they had been taught and stand fast on its promises. Life can be hard, especially when problems come from many directions at once. You may be facing one of the most difficult days of your life, but you have hope in the grace of God. And like Paul instructed the church at Corinth to do, you must remember the power of the Gospel and stand fast in it. "Stand fast" is another way of saying stay firm. Don't waiver in the midst of today's conflict. Don't let the situation make you think that you're going to lose.

You are a winner in Christ. No matter what the outcome today, ultimately God has promised though weapons and conflicts may come, they will not destroy us- "No weapon formed shall prosper against you in the end. And every tongue that rises against you, you shall condemn. (Isaiah 54:17). The day will come that the truth will come out. You will be vindicated but only when you follow righteousness. Your Savior's death was not in vain and when you trust in

God and follow His lead, he will not let you be put to shame.

Another translation for 1 Corinthians 16 says, "Stand firm in faith. Be courageous. Be strong." Verse 14 is the most important of all. Everything that we do should be done in love. It's the love of God in us that will keep us from anxiety and distress. 1 John 4:18 refers to the torment that fear and anxiety bring and tells us that perfect love casts out fear. The fear of daily struggles and challenges threaten to break us, but it's not until we make the choice to stand firm in our faith unwaveringly and walk in love, that we become the victorious.

In order to stand tall when the world tries to knock you down, you must first kneel before God, so He can lift you up.- Unknown

DAY 18 He Will Deliver You

But the Lord stood at my side and gave me strength, so that through me the message might be fully proclaimed and all the Gentiles might hear it. And I was delivered from the lion's mouth. 2 Timothy 4:17

Paul told Timothy about the first time he was arrested for preaching the gospel. When he went before the judge, he was alone. Everyone had abandoned him. I should note that he said, "…may it not be held against them". Paul went on to say, "But the Lord stood at my side…" We can say the same today. The Lord stands at our side in the times of trouble to be our protector and our deliverer. He gives us strength to endure under extreme pressure. Standing alone is difficult, but at some point in our lives, we may have to. And it's not a time for us to judge and condemn those who have left us. It's a time to lean heavily on the Lord for strength knowing that He has a plan for us that will ultimately bring us to victory and glorify the Kingdom. There is a message that God wants you to get to the world, "God is love." No matter how big the betrayal, we are Godly enough to rise above the pettiness of this world and be a light in darkness. There was a time in my life when I asked, "Why am I always the one who has to change, Lord? When are you going to do something about them?" It took a long time for me to realize that I am equipped with the grace to overcome. I have a power inside me that they do not have. We are strong in Christ. And because of that, the responsibility to keep the peace is mine. But I can do it through Jesus. If someone has left you alone, don't give it another thought. Don't allow the feelings of betrayal to distract you from the larger picture. Turn to the everlasting Father, El Olam. A person with a winning attitude accepts and understands that God has given us great responsibility to stand, sometimes alone, but by the same token we have assurance that He will be at our side to strengthen us.

Life may be tough but we have a God that is tougher. - unknown

DAY 19 You Have Supernatural Strength

Then he answered and spake unto me, saying, This is the
word of the LORD unto Zerubbabel, saying, Not by might,
nor by power, but by my spirit, saith the LORD of hosts.
Zechariah 4:6

This scripture should give us so much confidence. Not in
ourselves, but in the commitment of our Lord to give us
victory in life. Too often we focus on our own strength and
that makes us hesitant to take risks or push ourselves
beyond our physical, financial, or educational limitations.
A popular saying, "the sky is the limit" can be an
intimidating declaration to make for some. It's a great start
to say that, but still, the sky, in actuality is a limit. There is
something beyond this earth and sky that we see. There is a
heavenly Kingdom where all things are perfect and every
great power exists. And it is from that spiritual world that
our greatest strength and ability comes. Why rely only on
human strength when supernatural strength is available by
His spirit?

Don't limit yourself only to what you can do. It is vain for
us to worry about how things will get done because we are
focusing only on our own human ability. In scripture,
Zerubbabel was tasked of rebuilding the temple and was
concerned because the responsibility was so great in the
face of adversity. God told Zerubbabel that neither might

nor power would help him to accomplish his goal and overcome the adversity, but rather the spirit of God. You see it's wonderful to try your best and put your best foot forward. Our savior encourages diligence and excellence. And Psalm 90:17 says He will bless the work of our hands. But how much more can be accomplished through the power of the spirit that knows all, sees all, and knew you before you were even formed in your mother's womb? (Jeremiah 15). Even if there is a daunting task before you, don't limit yourself, but most important don't limit the possibilities of what the spirit can accomplish through a willing heart.

"Your life mainly consists of 3 things! What you think, What you say and What you do! So always be very conscious of what you are co-creating!" — Allan Rufus

DAY 20 What You Do For Him Matters

Therefore, my beloved brethren, be ye steadfast, unmovable, always abounding in the work of the Lord, forasmuch as ye know that your labor is not in vain in the Lord

1 Corinthians 15:58

In the microwave society that we live in, we want to see things happen fast, quick and in a hurry. When things are moving too slow, we tend to give up and move on to something else. But that's not always how God works. In my experience, more often than not, the Lord takes His time. It's during this time that our faith develops and we learn the power of perseverance. James 1:3 tells us the testing of our faith produces patience. This is how we receive the promises, through faith and patience (Hebrews 6:12). The worst thing we can do is become discouraged because things aren't happening fast enough.

Years ago, I had a good friend who worked in the ministry. She was very diligent in attending services, studying her lessons, and developing programs for various auxiliaries. But when the time came for praise to be given, she was always looked over. She didn't understand why her hard work wasn't being acknowledged. She talked to me about giving up. Her thought was, *since no one recognized her work, why should she do it?* I told my friend what I am telling you today. Her time spent teaching, planning, and coordinating was not in vain. And even though being overlooked was a hard pill to swallow, she shouldn't allow herself to become discourage. Man did not give her the talent to do what she had accomplished; they had simply reaped the benefits. As such she shouldn't seek their recognition or approval. But rather work enthusiastically for the glory of God. In short, her work was not in vain. And if she stood fast, she would be rewarded.

It's human nature to want to quit when things aren't going the way we want, as fast as we want. But in today's scripture, Paul encourages us stay fired up about everything that we do because none of it is in vain. Though it may seem that the desired results aren't manifesting and our work all for nothing. That is not true. Every good deed is rewarded but you can't give up. Keep pushing forward standing firm on the victory that you have already obtained through Christ Jesus.

"The venerable teachers, philosophers & spiritual practitioners throughout history have concluded that the greatest happiness we can experience comes from the development of an open, loving heart." — Allan Lokos

DAY 21 You Will Overcome

Ye are of God, little children, and have overcome them: because greater is he that is in you, than he that is in the world. 1 John 4:4

I'm not a big boxing fan, but I've watched a few matches. And *Rocky* is one of my absolute favorite movies of all time. It amazes me the pain that those two fighters are willing to endure round after round until one of them wins. Neither of them *really* knows who is going to win. But they still fight just as hard from start to finish. Ultimately one of them stands, gloves raised high, beaten but victorious, bruised but substantially wealthier.

Christians don't' literally step into the ring, but we do fight faith fights every single day. We fight against illness, emotional trauma, rebellious children, financial distress and the list goes on. All too often it feels that the outcome is uncertain. But encouraging words like 1 John 4:4, assure us that we've already won. The fight was fixed when Jesus rose from the dead. As long as we obediently respond to God's instruction and wise counsel we can't lose. Like a fighter has a trainer we have the Holy Spirit to guide us and lead us. We may have to go to the 12th round, but we will win. Jesus overcame the world and rose again victorious over sin and death. He went the distance to ensure our victory in life.

Go into your faith fight today with a winning attitude. Knowing that you have already won. And no matter what you will not lose. You may get knocked down, but you won't get knocked out. You may be bruised, but you will not be broken. And regardless of how many rounds your fight last, you will ultimately stand victorious, hands raised high, substantially wealthier in wisdom, knowledge, and joy!

"Positive attitude enables you to go with passion and see possibility in every challenging circumstance. It was by that, that great achievers picked up metal scraps on the floor and saw machines built from it." — Israelmore Ayivor

DAY 22 Be Encouraged

"For it is written, He shall give his angels charge over thee, to keep thee:" Luke 4:10

This is one of the most inspirational bible scriptures in the book of Luke. It shows God's love in the form of protection. I've prayed it over my sons on more than one occasion. Especially for my oldest, while we were standing in faith for his deliverance from addiction. And still today in prayer. But what I find most fascinating about this scripture is who is quoting it-Satan. Not one of the disciples, not Jesus, not a lay person, but the Devil himself during his attempt to talk Jesus into jumping off the highest point of the temple (4:9). The enemy wanted to stop Jesus from succeeding in his mission to redeem the world. So he tried to manipulate him through temptations.

There are times when the enemy may try to use the word against us. He will take what God says and try to bring on condemnation and make us believe that God is angry with us for something. The enemy will tempt us to quit in all manner of ways just as He tempted Christ to give up. Maybe you have a big dream and it's something you know will allow you to impact the lives of others in a positive way, but you're being tempted to give up. The enemy is telling you that the sacrifice is too great and your attempt is in vain.

Be encouraged though temptation to quit comes against you, you have already been equipped to overcome the temptation. James 4:7 says, "Resist the Devil and he will flee from you." And an even greater comfort comes from believing 1 Corinthians 10:13, *There hath no temptation taken hold of you but such as is common to man. But God is faithful; He will not suffer you to be tempted beyond that which ye are able to bear, but with the temptation will also make a way to escape, that ye may be able to bear it.* The devil is a liar. If God has placed a mission in your heart, then He will accomplish that good work in you (Psalm 138:8) if you don't allow Satan to distract you with his lies and temptations. Consider this, if the enemy seems to be working overtime to stop you that just might be an indication that you're closer to victory than you think. Whatever the sacrifice your dream requires, ask God for grace to endure. Trust God. Stay in prayer. And don't give up.

There are too many nay-sayers out there who will try to discourage you. Don't listen to them. The only one who can make you give up is yourself. - Sidney Sheldon

DAY 23 Be Ye Lifted Up!

"Lift up your heads, O ye gates; and be ye lift up, ye everlasting doors; and the King of glory shall come in. Who is this King of glory? The Lord strong and mighty, the Lord mighty in battle. " (Psalms 24:7-8)

The psalms remind us repeatedly to praise the Lord. When the Lord repeats His Word, it is to make you sit up and take notice. God deserves our praise. And it may seem that praising someone else isn't the best way to stay motivated and encouraged, but when it comes to your almighty God. Your savior, provider, banner, and protector, it's a different story. You can't help but be lifted up yourself! It's the powerful by-product of lifting your hands in adoration to the mighty Father. When you do, you stop focusing on your feelings and circumstances. You come into the presence of God and in His presence fear, anger, loss, and doubt must flee.

There was a time in my life when I suffered from depression. I was so down I had to make myself get out of bed and go to church on Sunday mornings. I felt tired and worn out. My heart was heavy, but when I lifted my hands during praise and worship something happened. The stress lifted. You see, when we glorify God and lift Him up; the devil flees because he hates praise. When the joy of the

Lord takes hold of you, you feel stronger, healthier and happier. *"For ye shall go out with joy and be led forth with peace; the mountains and the hills shall break forth before you into singing, and all the trees of the field shall clap their hands."* (Isa. 55:12) Now that's praise.

Praising God will lift you up. His everlasting, loving arms will envelope you as you stand in His presence. You don't have to be a professional singer, or have the perfect stance or sway. Just put on some praise music and lift your hands to the heavens. Give Him the praise He is due and be lifted up into a realm of joy, hope, love and ever-increasing faith. Let Him take control. Don't let your problems get you down. Look to the heavens from which your help comes (Psalm 121:1). And be lifted up!

DAY 24 Plant Your Victory Banner Ahead Of Time

"Be strong and of a good courage; be not afraid, neither be thou dismayed: for the Lord thy God is with thee withersoever thou goest." (Joshua. 1:9)

God commanded Joshua three times to be strong and have good courage and assured him of His constant presence if His commandments were obeyed. (Josh. 1:8-9) He promised that: "the eternal God is thy refuge, and underneath are the everlasting arms: and he shall thrust out the enemy from before thee; and shall say, Destroy them." (Deut. 33:27)

Knowing the Lord and obeying His commandments are the two main ingredients for the God kind of courage. Courage is defined as greatness of heart, spirit to meet danger, and boldness. El Shaddai, the All-Sufficient and Mighty One is on your side. He is Jehovah Nissi; the Lord, your Victory Banner. (Ex. 17:15) Think about that for a moment. Normally, a victory flag would be flown after a battle, but because God is our banner of victory, we can fly our victory flag as soon as a faith fight begins. Because of their obedience, Moses and Joshua were assured of God's presence in their time of need. Today we have the blessed assurance the greater One who lives in us. 1 John 4: says, "greater is He that is in you, than he that is in the world." We have to take our eyes off what is happening in front of us and focus on the greater spiritual battle that is taking place. And with the whole armor of God we can and will be victorious!

"Believing in negative thoughts is the single greatest obstruction to success."
- Charles F. Glassman

DAY 25 Blessed to Be a Blessing

We, as Christians, are consecrated, set apart, and highly favored. When God blesses us, it is more than houses, cars, and expensive jewelry. God's blessings are designed to make you stand out. You are peculiar. And what makes you peculiar is that you are chosen to be a royal, holy priest for Him. In this role you are to be a blessing, not only to those around you but first and foremost to Him, who has called you out of darkness into His glorious light. (1 Peter 3:9). You are consecrated, highly favor, a holy priest. You are awesome!

When you obey the voice of God and keep His commandments (Exodus 16:5-6), you will hear His voice and be able to lead your life in a manner that pleases Him and opens the doors for abundant blessings to flow in your life and through you to others around you. You see you're being positive blessed and highly favored isn't just about you; it's about helping to improve the outlook of others you come in contact with. When you put yourself in a position to be blessed and to be a blessing, God's blessing will come upon you and overtake you. Are you ready for blessings? Are you ready to abound in every area of your life; to have victory over your enemies and live peacefully and in good health? Of course you are. And God wants you to have all of these blessings. In Proverbs 8 17-21, the

Lord says, *"I love them that love me; and those that seek me early shall find me. Riches and honour are with me; yea, durable riches add righteousness. My fruit is better than gold; and my revenue than choice silver. I lead in the way of righteousness, in the midst of the paths of judgment; that I may cause those that love me to inherit substance; and I will fill their treasures."* Expect your share of blessings. They are ready to overtake you. Thank Him for them, and position yourself mentally, emotionally and physically to receive them.

"When life gives you lemons, you don't make lemonade. You use the seeds to plant a whole orchard - an entire franchise! Or you could just stay on the Destiny Bus and drink lemonade someone else has made, from a can." – Anthon St. Maarten

DAY 26 Give It to God

*How heavy are the burdens you're carrying? Are you
weighed down with a load of guilt, financial woes, an
abusive husband, or the death of a child? Jesus says: "My
yoke is easy, and my burden is light." (Matthew. 11:30)*

That almost sounds like a nice cliché, eh? You may be
thinking: "Yeah right! You don't know the problems I've
got!" I do know where you're coming from. I empathize as
I have some pretty tough ones too. But you know what?
We're not alone in this thing. When I get really pressed, I
encourage myself, "I can do all things through Christ who
strengthens me." (Philippians 4: 13). I encourage you to
stand on that verse, speak it every day, and during your
daily activities give your burdens to the Lord. There is a
song we used to sing when I was younger. The chorus
encouraged, "turn it over to Jesus. He can work it out."
Easier said than done your thinking, right? We have to
have faith to believe that God will solve everything. And
really give it to Him. Ask Him, *"Lord would you please
carry this burden for me as you promised you would?"* If
God promised, He will do it. He is not a man that he should
lie- ever. Lift your burdens up to Him, "Lord, I don't know
the answer. I can't bear this any longer." His Grace is

sufficient for you as His strength is made perfect in weakness. (2 Corinthians. 12:9) When you are weak, He is strong. When you let go and let God, you open the door to miracles and wonderful testimonies of His goodness in your life. Take off your heavy burdens. Let Him take care of them for you. It's His Promise, and He never fails!

Come unto me, all ye that labor and are heavy laden, and I will give you rest. Take my yoke upon you, and learn of me: for I am meek and lowly in heart: and ye shall find rest unto your souls. For my yoke is easy, and my burden light. (Matthew 11:28-30)

DAY 27 Your Persistence Is Powerful

And he spake a parable unto them to this end, that men ought always to pray, and not to faint; (Luke 18:1)

In Luke 18 verses 1-8 Jesus tells the disciples the story of a widow woman who was very persistent in her pursuit to obtain justice from a certain judge. Jesus shared this parable with the disciples to encourage them that they should continue to pray and never give up.

What's interesting about the judge in Luke 8 is that he was an unbeliever. The scripture said he did not fear "God or care about people". Many times in life we are dealing with people who could care less about our situations. Yet because they are in positions of authority, we are force to have to deal with them anyway. As believers we should not be afraid to face these kinds of people because we have a God who can turn the cold hearts of men and give us favor in every situation. Though the judge did not grant the widow justice the first time she requested it, she did not give up and walk away without hope. Instead she returned to the judge again and again.

There are times when it seems our request is being ignored. We pray and pray, but no answer-no results. This is not the time to tuck tail and walk away. Instead this is a time to press in-and stand firm. Because the widow woman did not give up and she was persistent in the pursuit of justice for her case, the judge granted her justice. It's important to note that the judge did not grant the widow justice because he cared about her or because he was a man of God with compassion. The judge gave her what she wanted because she was persistent. There is power in persistence. If an unrighteous judge can grant a petition surely our God who loves us dearly will grant our petition as well. Though it seems we are not receiving an answer from God, don't give up. Keep praying and keep going before Him with your requests. Read Luke 18 for encouragement. Remain faithful that you will receive justice and your petition will be granted. In the dictionary persistence is defined as "Firm or obstinate continuance in a course of action in spite of difficulty or opposition". Whether the request is for business success; a family matter; or a health concern, stay your course of faith regardless of the difficulty you face. Keep going before God with a good attitude. He loves you and hears your cry. But you must not give up. Your faith and persistence has power!

Calvin Coolidge the 30th president of the United States understood the principle of persistence, *"Nothing in this world can take the place of persistence. Talent will not; nothing is more common than unsuccessful people with talent. Genius will not; unrewarded genius is almost a proverb. Education will not; the world is full of educated derelicts. Persistence and determination alone are omnipotent. The slogan "press on" has solved and always will solve the problems of the human race"*

DAY 28 You Have A Bright Future

For I know the thoughts that I think toward you, saith the LORD, thoughts of peace, and not of evil, to give you an expected end.- Jeremiah 29: 11

Whatever you're going through right now may be really weighing you down. It's easy to get discouraged and think that what you believe for is never going happen. But take courage. God is mindful of you and He says in Jeremiah that He has a plan for you. You are His creation and He knows you better than you know yourself. As you seek Him in your daily comings and goings, trust that He will guide you in the direction you need to go to reach your ultimate place of glory.

Naturally, it can be difficult at times to remain enthusiastic about your journey. Perhaps you feel like you are on a path that doesn't make any sense. You thought that you would reach your goal by going down a different path. And the path you're on seems to be leading to nowhere positive. It is vital that you do not lose courage during these times of uncertainty. God's ways are not our ways and some days you will be confounded by what is happening. But trust Him. Remember He knows the ending from the beginning. Who better to guide you than someone who knows what is going to happen in the end?

Take heart in His words "I know the thoughts I think toward you...thoughts of peace, and not evil, to give you an expected end. God does not have evil intent. His desire for you is that you succeed and realize the glorious potential that He has placed in you from the beginning. God knew that you would be facing this struggle long before it happened. Trust Him and know that in His good plan this present circumstance will work together for your good. He has already devised a way for you to get through this dark time and as you go through it know that you are on your way to your bright future!

"Keep your head up, your faith strong, and your eyes open for the little miracles all around you...because they are there, just waiting to be discovered." – *Mandy Hale*

DAY 29 Your Life May Be a Mess…But Grace!

"Let us then approach God's throne of grace with confidence, so that we may receive mercy and find grace to help us in our time of need." Hebrews 4:16

Though God has this bright future planned for you, there are things you need to do to ensure that you reach your place of destiny in life. The enemy wants to keep you from your destiny by keeping you focused on the mistakes of your past, but GRACE has you covered. Don't waste another day over thinking your "shortcomings", "flaws", and "sins". Instead, meditate on the word and keep your heart and mind filled with the inspiration of the Holy Spirit. Study day and night so that you will know what God's word has to say about your present and your future.

God promises if you do this, you will make your way prosperous and you will have good success. (Joshua 1:8) Let the Holy Spirit be your guide in all that you do. Ask for guidance so that you know that the path you are taking to reach your destiny is ordained by God. Keep the words of your mouth in line with the word of God's gospel. It will transform your life. Romans 1:16 says *the Gospel is the power of God.* Don't be ashamed to declare it over your life daily.

Always have an attitude of gratitude and grace. Extend forgiveness to others and know in your heart that God is extending that same grace and forgiveness to you. You are fearfully and wonderfully made (Psalm 139:14) in God's image.

"Happiness cannot be traveled to, owned, earned, worn or consumed. Happiness is the spiritual experience of living

every minute with love, grace, and gratitude." –Denis Waitley

DAY 30 Shout With A Voice of Triumph

When David faced Goliath he shouted: "Thou comest to me with a sword, and with a spear; but I come to thee in the name of the Lord of Hosts, the God of the armies." Your problems and challenges are no match for the Lord of Hosts. You must believe with all your heart and never doubt that God would deliver you. Just like David believed that His God would deliver him from Goliath. No matter how big the giant or how many people are telling you that the giant is too big to conquer, stand and declare victory.

Use the word (scripture) that God has placed in your heart and speak victory; put on your spiritual armor; plant your victory banner; and continue to pray without ceasing. As you claim your victory daily, refuse to allow people and circumstances around you to cause you to lose faith. When doubt tries to come and steal your faith, arrest it with the word of God. Declare that you and your house will serve the Lord.

"Be strong and of a good courage; be not afraid, neither be thou dismayed: for the Lord thy God is with thee withersoever thou goest." (Josh. 1:9)

PERSONAL THOUGHTS AND REFLECTIONS

PERSONAL THOUGHTS AND REFLECTIONS

PERSONAL THOUGHTS AND REFLECTIONS

PERSONAL THOUGHTS AND REFLECTIONS

Additional Books You May Enjoy

If you were blessed by this book and feel that the message would help others, please take a moment and leave a brief comment on Amazon.com. Your comments really make a difference. God bless

Read More Books In Lynn's By Faith I Declare Series:

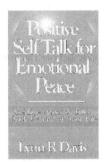

Positive Self Talk For Emotional Peace: Set Boundaries and Take Back Control of Your Life

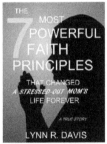

The 7 Most Powerful Faith Principles That Changed A Stressed-Out Mom's Life Forever

Made in the USA
Las Vegas, NV
05 December 2020